The Woods

Something unseen
Lurks beyond the trees

Deep within the thicket
Quieting the crickets

Cool is the twilight breeze,
that often slowly stirs
the decaying leaves

Something surreal
hides silently
within the shadows

Cracking the branch
silencing the sparrows

Something very frightening and unknown
was seen in the woods
early one morning
a newly formed creature

Exiting from beyond the shady trees
swiftly crossing on a lonely dark
unknown
back road

On Bordellos

on bordello heels, she smiles
the instance of an innocent child
devours the edges of a man soul
the perfumed imagination, now slips
into her elusively moistened lips

gaze of
accentuated amber
whiplashes the horse in
belly dancer swirl-winds

karma sutra fringe
slender painted tips
levitate above the red glow
sliding down
sliding down
the crystal splashed
brass pole

disheveled masculine dominance- swivels
within a tables turn, head spinning, like a soft brass
top
the smashed ego drowns in rounds of alcohol
warmed by static friction, so easily melted, finally into
flowing currency

JAZZ

Pearls and Opals
    Amber and Sandstones
Emeralds
    Diamonds
        Rubies
            Sapphires

Stir swizzle sticks

Crystallized reconfigurations
        Of protons and neutrons
      Dug from the earth
        Made from water
          Heat and
            Pressure

        Facets of mud
    Now gathered to dance
      within night shades

      defying   gravity

Soft and slow, dancing with,
    Euclidian geometry
        Newton's tangent rainbows
    Darwin's enigmas
        Van Gogh's lost Ear

Answers flow in and out in ~ quantum
waves ~
Defying probability

Mandela's guts and wisdom
Reverberate within Coltrane's Sax
Jazz notes astound
and exist
for
mere seconds
but somehow remain
arousing resonance
until dawn

When the wild spirits sleep
profound...

Night Café

The hordes arrive early
        For bad coffee
    Line forms
            As if a new religion was born

    Time is a blur
            As the burnt hash browns stir

    Mascara bleeds into
            Thrift shop fur and leather jackets
seams

    French fry ketchup drench, soon the
            Lipstick cigarette need, quenched in
it.

        Cleavage has easily found
        Another bulge in town

    The lonely old man in from the cold
            Sits and stares above another coffee
bone

        Aggravated waitress smiles above sore feet
        Ripped nylons, wrinkled eyes, broken
dreams

Newly formed lovers interlock like
pretzels
Necking, rubbing, laughing, stroking inside
Red booths

Asshole drunks make a scene; Swearing,
Fighting, Yelling!
Then falling asleep…snoring…fading
allegory…

Grease splashed cook, looks up, from behind a
square hole, slams down
ceramic plate, always on the go, guest ticket carousel
spins into "Orders up!" winds

In the corner hides a poet;
Coffee, pen, napkin,
Just quietly observing…

More Coffee

Doughnut shop
Cops
Lawyers
Politicians
College kids
All with burnt morning tongues

Swish
Swash
Spilling
Sipping
Dripping
The steaming
Brew

Hyper kinetic drooling

The black aromatic fueling
Drives the overdrive
Of the mad bee hive
Losing sleep at night
pharmaceutical giants delight

Lined up and,
Waiting…
In the grog
Waiting...
Standing in the fog
Waiting….

For an overpriced corporate dosing
Waiting…..
In front of the counter
Waiting…waiting…waiting…

At the vending machine line….Inside the airport
concourse line…Lined up…

at the street corner café.
In the cold, in the rain,
or on a hot summer's day…Lined up,
at the
roach coach, outside the homeless shelters, alone at home,
in front of the percolating plastic gurgling metronome,
waiting…
waiting, at the office, in the break room,
still waiting…all
lined up…
for that more of that morning cup…

Beneath the Neon Sign

beneath the moon
neon sign, door, saloon

return to the womb
darken room, ambient red

happy hour blooms
worlds hide behind

doors, beneath neon signs, hide
masqueraders, entranced spirals

gently sedated desolation
superficial joy gathers

wounded brain stem
eaten by the worm

friends, strangers
laughing, watching

serrated, wry, barkeep
liquid ghost dealer

Toast to life!
Prost to buttered minds!
Cheers to deaf ears!
Solute to the Juke!

music is the rudder
 swaying sea legs

yeast, smoke, perfume
 high heels, balloons

we can now discuss
 the evening news

speculating, dissecting
 television frogs

About Money

How money has no soul
memory or passion

Strange how this jaded
Configuration

Creates the illusion
of importance

Geed, another well soiled seed
growing fat on the bar stool

Absorbed in pecking
at the cell phone keys

How money
loves friends

How friends love,
 mansions, speed boats

The bank loves
them too

How money
will never tell you

Just what you know
is nothing

Until you know
what nothing

Really is

Intersections

We brush
each other
  swiftly
slight glances
  avoiding
near collisions

some politely smile
  some oddly stare, some just thinking only
of only themselves-- as we intersect there

  intertwining mists of music
wind through the naked air there

  swirling amongst busty street walkers
      jugglers on unicycles
        young boys hosted atop
          fathers' broad shoulders

  the smell of bratwurst, onions, French fries,
      evaporates from diners on wheels
rudely clashing with perfume, armpit sweat and burnt
gas

a pregnant woman in heels pushes a double stroller
      past an old veteran in a wheel chair
dirty plastic cup, miniature billboard, amputee

Lazy henchmen patrol, with squawking sirens
  now and then, silver emblem of audacity

beneath the waves of twisting
    red and blues lights
encapsulating evil doer mobiles
       inside long moments of silence,
panic, anger, fear, frustration, and regret

Yellow cab edges by
like a three toed sloth
  eating a banana

     Coagulated
painted alloyed beasts,
  screech, squeal,
howl, moan and
      drool like panting dogs

breathing   consuming
  energy   paused
poised   waiting

  waiting, drooling
    waiting…panting…waiting
to taste the precious freedom
     of motion once again

waiting for the stern
   bright red circular
cursor to jump through
   transient yellow alarm
back to green liberty

seems at the intersection

we are controlled
and manipulated
by our own designs

Cathedrals

can humility
  transcend through
  stained windows,
    mosaic scenes ?

   grace
    watching
   from corner saints

    gargoyles
     remind of things
      that hide in the shadows
       watching,
         watching,
            poised
        with frozen wings

     the brass baritone bell
     sings to the Lord above,
            beneath,
       within,
         in-between

     the pipe organ calls
     us earthly creatures
       -in throughout-
     the large archway
        doors
         that sway
       into incense clouds

we stand up
we sing aloud
we pray
we sit down
 beneath the shroud

the conical, jagged
towers,
        reaching,
                reaching,
                        into heaven
stretching the shadow of the crucifix tip

The cruel life of Dogs

  dogs have souls
dreams and love with
a pounding
heart beat

dogs have
loyalty
compassion
guts
kindness
inquisitiveness
respect
dignity
zest

a stomach that growls
and tongue that drools
at that smell of distant food

the desire to run within the wind
and play inside the sunshine, like a pup

most other dogs they meet
they either want to bite
lick or screw

dogs and men
are much alike
in many ways, they say

dogs may be better
than men
in many ways, if I may

for we are much too hostile
and way too messy

The Maintenance Man

Early morning
radio is talking
familiarity is
comforting

coffee warms
  the belly well,
 stirs the senses, as
the reflection in
the mirror is brushed,
 and shaved under
  the whiskey weir

forearms, biceps
like jackhammers
hands worn like bear traps,
outside, it's starting to rain
but a strong man don't complain

make the sandwich now
 put hard boiled egg
chips and pickle
into the bag.

let the dog out
into the yard, through
the back door for the day

top thermos off
in the mind, start to pray,
gonna be another
   Long day

pass the casino
the bar
the graveyard

5: 45 am, on the way.

ride down the road, across
that lonesome brown river,
the spewing stacks, emerge
as the dawn is beginning
to crack

through the gate
flash the badge
flannel shirt, jeans,
boots, day dreams,
put on the hard
hat, need the cash
no turning back.

One for the Cats

Hey why not?
No one ever mentions
Them anymore

Because all they
Seem to do
Is stare out
the window
at the dogs and the
other cats, and the
sparrows flying by

making strange,
hisses and meows, while
squinting their eyes

frankly,
no one knows,
 nor understands,
just quite why

they don't seem
to want too much
but then everything
when they wish it so

as if they are not sure
at first, but suddenly
ready to go

finicky creatures, sleek,

pampered, calculating,
sharp claws and teeth

they know how to
pick the good meat from the bowl
or off the edge of the street

most cats are smarter than they look
and most have mysterious souls

sometimes for some
unknown reason
they just disappear

no meows for some time
just a few trinkets in a box
left behind

they tell me a good
cat comes back
within a few days

they say you'll know then,
somewhere in your head,
the cat was really yours,

and you'll be amazed,
especially, after negotiating
this crazy maze

that just when you feared
your cat may have been dead

you'll wake up
one morning
and find it laying
        and purring
right there in your bed

The Chronic Condition

You don't understand
the dimensions of
my window

They were given to me
by natural philanthropy

I'd tell you the reason
for this chronic condition
but I'm sworn to secrecy

To uphold the law hidden
inside the agenda of talons

To answer these questions
that baffle and haunt
your superstitious lost souls
 encircled in static whispers…

You'll never know the lights
of aurora borealis nights
inside dreams that transmit
and transcend the plaster

Ceiling fans swirling your
adolescent fodder into the
alien walls that protect
the lining of the womb

You'll never know the
Bottom of my soul

Nor the subtle worm that
burrows the brain stem
searching the lines of code

staring out the from behind
the maroon felt curtain seam

you'll never understand
by watching as the incongruent
folds sway behind the constructed pane

Night Shades

The night shades
            knows
                    sex
                        knows
                                freedom
                                    knows
                                        sublime

    longing
            desire
        thirst
                art
                    passion

        Lust!
            Eros!
                Pathos…
                . Bathos….
                        Climax!!
                            Rebirth!!!

        Predator
                    knows
                            prey

            the trial is still warm…

Almost Nothing

Superficial whale
   sing the tale of the song
       you sing to your young now

  We know what it is
  The idea of the idea
  Was always there, deep in the belly
    Sifted from the salt of the ocean
    Illuminated like a heard of angels

   What remains of the day?
   A Metropolis in the Bay
    Fog appears like
     Heavens clouds
     Cleaves the edges
      Of lazy mountains
       Dissolves the sides of
       Old stories, leaving only
        Crowns and pinnacles, to
         Attach us to our buried legends

    Did the moment know me long enough?
   For my head not to travel further than my feet

Was it an idea that always existed that brought me back
to the streets?

    Were you always bound to find me?
     And I to discover you, somehow too?

Do we know enough now to Stop.

And not say another word…

….for the day may wither much too soon

To realize the truth is almost nothing

Everything I ever needed is right here, in
you.

They

How hard it is to live in this form
to exist as a host to the parasite
that surrounds us, sucks our blood

feeds like a worm inside the apple
laughing, belly full, making love to itself

How hard it is to find freedom within
when all they want from you, is always
less, than they really want to take

One day you wake to know, they
are nothing more than slippery snakes

and you are nothing more than a meal

being slowly digested, inside their guts
silently stripped of verve

So you give a little more, to survive the cataclysm,
and they take a little more back, and so then

you try to hide something for yourself
conceal it, fold it, tuck it away, in between the pages

of an old novel, lost on a dusty worn sagging
wooden shelve, termite bitten, beer and coffee stained

wrinkled, a crumpled road map, nearly forgotten
the edges just peaking out, buried in dank obscurity

squeezed somewhere in-between

How often it is now that they stay and read, taking
nothing more than the thoughts within the stashed page

Most seem to only pick the pretty books, everybody's
read,
seemingly clean, binding never really cracked, dazzling
colors

impressive cover art, expensive press, quite an act to
follow
that stampede over the canons edge, only to hear their
vain echo's

Infinite Loop

The dividing cell

The grocery line

Chopsticks that
Swirl on the wall

Claws that scratch
the crooked branch
harboring the nest
of honey bees

the worm cut
by the tractor blade
and the crow
whose belly is full

The gruel on the
morning stool
the stumble and fumble
with the razor blade game

Battlefields of decisions
crossroads of collisions

Winding back roads
the squashed toad

opossum's blood
splattered carcass

left of center strip

The waiting room

The miraculous cries of birth

Velocity

that ethereal song was almost gone

before the anchored mystery shouted

over the distance through the e t h e r

the distance was never too long

for the mystery to dull over

that tangent s t r e t c h from the

recoiling spring of electromagnetism

the ghost parade was too long

to enjoy the night carnivals full extent

ferris wheels   blue ponies   roller coasters

masterfully driven by the mystifying

bones   s t r e t c h e d   and honed

with centripetal muscles of   torn heart

windings   generated from pine wood

Luck and the Miracle Mile

the longing turbine blades, that lazily swirled

silent claws scratching the cold morning wind

naked were the twisted trees, silent rings

hidden years of knowledge, dew drops

surreptitiously appearing on the fine edge

of sturdy limbs, as the towns languid streets

warm afternoon lost back roads, crossed by

county trunks, vacant sun bleached dairy farms

guarded by lethargically dreaming evergreen

spectators, distant dark interiors, nestling

the senses of concealed forest creatures

proud hawk pierces the dense blue sky

floating high over icy manure tilled soil

mounds of chunky snow, mysteriously appear

 atop the jagged grey lonesome shore stones

soft ice, shyly brushed with old snow, hides

the drama unfolding beneath the shallows of

the struggling ecosystem, now edges in her anger

her complex frustration, accelerates the melting

the currents begin to rise into an alluring crescendo

graciously saturating the condition of the ebbing heart

Stir Sticks

Poison voices
Slip in agony
Through salted
Night air

My hammock
Is bloating
Sagging
In the hips

Position   yourself
        in truth
Distance   yourself
   From   longing
Relive   yourself
                  Through
        Curling toes

Chaos
    In the trees
Bashful red
            Forest
Neon
    Maneuvers
through
    lavender
          leaves

Don't mind
Us

We refuges
              lost
woodland creatures
    bohemian demur
crouching
      beneath
a subtle moon
    taking a nap
in the red
        glow
on sticky
  wood

Shadows

Outside
some remained

In the haze
in the grey

sun pokes
clouds above

distant stacks
poison smoke

horns and sirens

BLARE
rubber neckers
stare…

At the tragedy
of the wreckage

bent and twisted
smashed and cracked

over there
where
bashful sun has passed
over the shattered glass
dirt smudged facades
blood spattered souls
arranged in the shadows

Lunar Iguana

This is what was ignored
This is what was denied

Food on the plate balled in a napkin
or fed to the dog, hand under the table

Daring snippets

Fill empty spaces

Empty chair stares

Compressed
Steel wound
Coiled dreams

Animated gamers

Valiant shields

Formidable blades

Metaphysical

Lunar iguana

Snaps it tail

Slips from slimy green
jaded shore stones as

Moonlight ripples,
sparkles, lighting the runway

To delve into the vast horizon
bounded by stars and obscurity

Into the heavens, buoyantly guarded
by ancient gamers;

Gods, fearsome warriors, scorpion hearts, mystical
monkeys,
kissing fish, snake eyes, dragon souls, bull horns and
languid reptiles

www.ingramcontent.com/pod-product-compliance
Lightning Source LLC
Chambersburg PA
CBHW030309030426
42337CB00012B/646

* 9 7 8 0 6 1 5 9 7 7 6 4 5 *